MW01102443

Soccer Crazy

Shey Kettle

illustrated by
Meredith Thomas

MACMILLAN

First published in 2008 by
MACMILLAN EDUCATION AUSTRALIA PTY LTD
15–19 Claremont Street, South Yarra 3141

Visit our website at www.macmillan.com.au or
go directly to www.macmillanlibrary.com.au

Associated companies and representatives throughout the world.

National Library of Australia
Cataloguing-in-Publication data

Kettle, Shey.
  Soccer crazy.

  For primary school students.
  ISBN 978 1 4202 6144 8 (pbk.).
  ISBN 978 1420262179 (set 3)

  1. Soccer – Juvenile fiction. I. Title. (Series: Girlz
  rock!).

A 823.4

Series created by Felice Arena and Phil Kettle
Project management by Limelight Publishing Services Pty Ltd
Cover and text design by Lore Foye
Illustrations by Meredith Thomas

Printed in China

GIRLZ ROCK!

Contents

Carly   Mai

CHAPTER 1

The Weekend at Last!

Mai and Carly are walking home from school together. They're both really excited because it's Friday. And everyone knows that Friday means two things—the school week has finished and the weekend has started.

Mai "I love weekends."

Carly "Yeah, so do I."

Mai "So, what are we going to do?"

Carly (kicking an empty drink can)
"Let's practise our soccer skills."

Mai "Why?"

Carly "'Cause I watched the school
soccer team train today and I want
to be on the team."

Mai "But there are only boys on the school soccer team."

Carly "So? I think we're as good as them, and I think we should be on the team too!"

Mai "Yeah, but they probably won't let us be on the team."

Carly "Well, I reckon if we're good enough, they'll just have to let us."

Mai (laughing) "I think we'd need to be better than all of them, maybe even as good as Beckham."

Carly "Come on Mai, we should try. I know that I'm as good as they are—maybe even better!"

Mai "Okay! If you're game to try out for the team, then so am I."

Carly "Right. Let's start now. We can practise our passing with this can."

Carly and Mai take it in turns to kick the empty drink can. They kick it to each other, as if they are passing a soccer ball. The girls stop when they come to the park.

Carly "Hey! This is where we should come and practise."

Mai "What about the Hoover boys next door?"

Carly "You mean Joel and Jarred Hoover Vacuum-Cleaner? What about 'em?"

Mai "Well, we don't want them to come and play while we're here."

Carly "I'll just tell them that we've come to give them a big fat kiss— that'll soon scare them off."

Mai and Carly laugh.

Mai "What'll we wear?

Carly "Let's borrow some gear from
our brothers. They're not playing a
game tomorrow."

Mai "Great idea. Let's not tell them
though, or they might laugh at us."

The girls agree to meet the next
morning.

CHAPTER 2

Looking Good

Mai and Carly arrive at the park at nine o'clock the next morning. Both girls are dressed in soccer gear they've secretly taken from their brothers' wardrobes.

Mai "Wow! You look just like a professional player."

Carly "So do you!"

Mai "If the school coach could see us he'd put us on the team right now."

Carly (laughing) "I think that he'd want to see us play first."

Mai "Well, we should start training."

Carly "Great idea, but we're missing something."

Mai "What?"

Carly "A soccer ball."

Mai "I thought you had one."

Carly "Well, I thought you had one."

Mai "So, we look like real players, we talk like real players—but we haven't got a soccer ball."

Mai "Maybe we can pretend that we're kicking and head-butting a ball."

Carly "I think we need to train with a proper ball if we're going to be good enough to get on the school team."

Mai "Yeah, you're right."

Carly "Any ideas?"

Mai "I know what we can do."

Carly "What?"

Mai "We can go next door and ask the Hoover boys if we can use their soccer ball."

Carly "But if we do that, then they'll know we're playing here, and what's worse, they might want to play."

Carly and Mai sit on the ground
looking at each other, until Mai
jumps up.

Mai "I've got a plan!"
Carly "What? What's your plan?"
Mai "Well, first I've got to run home
    and get something. You wait here."

Mai runs home as fast as she can.

CHAPTER 3

Trust Me!

In a couple of minutes Mai returns
holding something small in her hand.

Carly "So, what have you got there?"
Mai "I've got something that will
  make sure that the Hoover boys
  won't want to play soccer with us."

Carly "What? Show me. Come on, show me."

Mai "Shut your eyes and I'm going to put it on you. And when I do, I'm sure those Hoover boys won't want to come near us."

Carly hesitates, then shrugs her shoulders and shuts her eyes.

Carly "I hope you know what you're doing."

Mai "Trust me."

Carly "That's what you said when I asked you not to tell Joel Hoover that I liked him."

Mai "He forced me to tell."

Carly "Yeah, right!"

Carly shuts her eyes. Mai uses a red lipstick to cover Carly's face with little red dots. Soon Carly looks like she has a really bad red-spot disease.

Mai "Now we can go and ask the Hoover boys for a loan of their soccer ball, 'cause when they see your face, there's no way they'll want to come and play with us in the park."

Carly "Great, but I don't want to ask them unless I can put lipstick dots on your face, too."

Mai agrees. Soon, Carly stands back and admires her handiwork.

Carly "Okay, now we're good. Let's go and ask them for the ball."

CHAPTER 4

Red-spot Disease

The girls knock on the Hoover boys'
door. They hear a vacuum cleaner being
turned off. When Joel Hoover opens the
door, he steps backwards quickly and
trips over the vacuum cleaner. He tells
the girls not to come any closer.

Carly "Hey, Joel, you look like you've just seen a ghost."

Mai "Yeah Joel, haven't you ever seen anyone with the very contagious red-spot disease before?"

Carly "Don't worry, we won't come too close, because if we breathe on you, you'll get the same bad red-spot disease."

Mai "And if you get the same disease as us, then you won't be able to play in the school soccer team."

Carly "So there!"

Mai "All we want is to borrow your soccer ball."

Carly "Yeah! And if you don't let us use your soccer ball, we might have to breathe all over you."

Keeping his distance, Joel throws his soccer ball to the girls. He tells them that they'll never be any good at soccer because they are girls.

Carly "You haven't seen us play. We're better than you and your brother. We could beat you any day."

Mai "Yeah! We could beat you, even with the bad red-spot disease."

The girls go back to the park and
start kicking and head-butting the
soccer ball.

Mai "Gee, I reckon that soccer is a
pretty easy game. All you've got to
do is kick the ball."

Carly "Yeah! Watch me, I bet I can
kick the ball from one end of the
park to the other."

Carly kicks the ball. It really does go from one end of the park to the other.

Mai "Now watch me! I'm going to dribble!"

Carly (giggling) "Boys are really good at dribbling. Ha! Mostly down the front of their shirts."

Mai "And here come the two best dribblers ever!"

CHAPTER 5

We're the Best

Joel and his brother Jarred are walking
towards the girls. They're dressed in
their soccer gear, but they look like
they've come from outer space.

Carly (laughing) "So what do you two
   think you're doing?"

Mai "And why are you wearing those underwater masks and snorkels?"

The boys mumble that they want to play soccer, but they don't want to catch the red-spot disease.

Carly "Well, I think that we can play a game with you, as long as you keep wearing those masks."

Mai "Yeah, but only if you promise that if we beat you, you won't laugh when we try out for the school soccer team."

The boys nod in agreement.

Carly "Let's have a goal kick-off. Whoever misses first, loses."

Mai "Great idea! We go first because we're sick, and because we're girls."

The girls move two rubbish bins to mark off a goal area.

Carly "I'll go first."

Carly puts the soccer ball on the ground and then runs and kicks it as hard as she can. The soccer ball flies between the bins. The girls jump up and down with excitement.

Mai "Great kick! We're one up. It's your turn, Hoover boys."

Jarred lines the ball up to take his kick. He moves in to kick and then stops and mumbles something.

Mai (looking at Carly) "What's he trying to say?"

Carly "Not sure, but I think his goggles have fogged up. Maybe he can't see anything."

Mai "Gee, Jarred, that's bad luck about your goggles fogging up. But if you don't take your kick, then we're the winners."

Carly "And if you miss the goal, guess what? We win anyway!"

Joel mumbles about having girls on the school soccer team. Jarred runs at the ball and kicks. The soccer ball zooms though the air, missing the goal, and over the fence into the boys' backyard.

Carly "Wow, look at it go!"
Mai "Pity it missed the goal."

Mai and Carly roll around laughing.

Carly "So boys, you lost! We won! We're the champions and you're the losers—and now you don't get to laugh when we try out for the school soccer team on Monday."

Mai "We'll see you later then. It's time for us to go home and wash the lipstick off our faces."

Carly "Don't forget to finish the vacuuming and to collect your soccer ball in case it rains."

Mai "So, boys, we look forward to seeing you at soccer training next week."

Carly "And don't forget—Girlz Rock at soccer!"

Mai

GIRLZROCK!
Soccer Lingo

Carly

dodging When one player moves quickly away from another player. If you are a good dodger, players in the other team will find it hard to keep up with you.

dribble To move the ball along the ground by running and kicking it to yourself.

goalkeeper The person who tries to stop the other team from getting goals.

header When a player uses their head to pass the ball to another player or to have a shot at goal.

high five When a player slaps the open hand of a team mate, especially to celebrate scoring a goal.

GIRLZ ROCK!
Soccer Must-dos

☆ Check that your boots have studs—
you don't want slip over when you're
running or trying to kick the ball.

☆ Clean your soccer boots before you
play. You'll always play better in clean
soccer boots. And if you don't, at
least you'll look a lot better.

☆ Make sure you wear a hair tie if you
have long hair. There is nothing worse
than trying to kick the ball when your
hair is in front of your eyes.

☆ If you want to be a really good
soccer player then you have to eat
healthy food and do regular training.
Remember, if you keep on training,
you'll play better soccer.

☆ Make sure that you always watch the ball when you are kicking it.

☆ Always shake the hands of the opposing team before the game starts and after the game finishes. And if you win, smile a lot.

☆ Learn to kick the soccer ball with both feet. It will help make you a really good player.

☆ Never talk back to the referee. If you do, you might end up getting a penalty for your team.

☆ And remember the most important rule in playing sport is "Make sure you always enjoy the game".

GIRLZ ROCK!
Soccer Instant Info

⚽ Soccer came from England. It is now played in more countries around the world than any other team sport.

⚽ The first international game of soccer was played between Scotland and England in 1872. The score was 0–0.

⚽ Soccer is played on a rectangular field with a goal area and net at each end.

⚽ You score a soccer goal by kicking or heading the ball over your opponents' goal line at the end of the field.

⚽ In soccer, each goal you score is worth one point.

 A soccer team has eleven players.

 The goalkeeper is the only player who is allowed to touch the ball with their hands.

 David Beckham is a world-famous English soccer player.

 The Australian women's soccer team is called the Matildas, and the Australian men's soccer team is called the Socceroos.

GIRLZ ROCK!
Think Tank

1 Can anyone play on a soccer team?

2 How many players in a soccer team?

3 If a soccer player dribbles, does that mean he or she moves the soccer ball with their feet or that they dribble down the front of their shirt?

4 Are goalkeepers allowed to touch the ball with their hands?

5 Who's the best at soccer, Australia or England?

6 How many points do you score if you get a goal?

7 Is David Beckham a soccer player or a singer?

8 If you head the ball into the goal, do you score a goal?

Answers

8 Yes, if you head the ball into the goal it counts as a goal.

7 A soccer player ... but apparently he sings really well in the shower!

6 You score one point if you score a goal.

5 Australia is the best at soccer, of course!

4 Yes. Goalkeepers are allowed to touch the ball with their hands.

3 It means both, but probably in a soccer game it means he or she moves the ball with their feet.

2 There are eleven players in a soccer team.

1 Yes! Anyone who is good enough at soccer can play on a team.

How did you score?

- If you got all 8 answers correct, then maybe you should be playing soccer for your country.

- If you got 6 answers correct, you might need to do some more training before trying out for a team.

- If you got fewer than 4 answers correct, then maybe you should think of playing another sport altogether.

Hey Girls!

I hope that you had as much fun reading my story as I had writing it. I loved reading and writing stories when I was young. And in the stories that I wrote, I was always better than I actually was in real life. It was great fun!

At school, why don't you use "Soccer Crazy" as a play, and you and your friends can be the actors. You can dress up in your soccer gear. Don't forget to bring your soccer ball and soccer boots, and if your school has a stage, you can pretend that it is a soccer field.

So ... have you decided who's going to be Mai and who's going to be Carly? And who's going to kick off? Make sure that you only pretend to kick off, or else you might get into trouble.

Make sure that you take this story home and get someone to read it out loud to you, or even act out the parts with you.

Reading at home is lots of fun and really important!

And remember, Girlz Rock!

Shey Kettle.

GIRLZ ROCK!
When We Were Kids

Shey

Holly

Shey talked to Holly, another *Girlz Rock!* author.

Holly "Were you a good soccer player when you were young?"

Shey "Yeah, I was pretty good."

Holly "Did you like heading the ball?"

Shey "No, heading the ball can hurt your head."

Holly "So, what were you best at when playing soccer?"

Shey "I was a great kicker."

Holly "How great?"

Shey "I once kicked a ball 10 kilometres."

Holly "Wow! How did you do that?"

Shey "It was good luck! I kicked the ball and it went over the fence and landed in the back of a moving truck."

GIRLZ ROCK!
What a Laugh!

Q Why did the soccer ball quit the team?

A Because it got sick of being kicked around!

GIRLZROCK!

Read about the fun that girls have in these **GIRLZROCK!** titles:

Birthday Party Bedlam

Pony Club

Doubles Trouble

Soccer Crazy

Dance Fever

Minigolf Face-off

Trapeze Dreams

Two at the Zoo

... and 20 more great titles to choose from!